HUMANS FOR SALE

ARIA DEEMIE

This is a work of fiction. All names, characters, places, and incidents are a product of the author's imagination. Any resemblance to real events or persons, living or dead, is entirely coincidental.

Published by Akashic Books

ISBN: 978-1-63614-248-7

Printed in China
First printing

EU Authorized Representative details:
Easy Access System Europe
Mustamäe tee 50, 10621 Tallinn, Estonia
gpsr.request@easproject.com

Akashic Books
Instagram, X, Facebook: AkashicBooks
info@akashicbooks.com
www.akashicbooks.com

African Poetry Book Fund
Brown University
10 Prospect Street
Box A
Providence, RI 02912

TABLE OF CONTENTS

PREFACE

by Sherry Shenoda

In *Humans for Sale*, Liberian poet Aria Deemie offers a journalist's clear-eyed analysis, along with a poet's attention to the intricacies of human relationships, and arrives at an integral whole. As though written in flight from great danger, Deemie turns her poet's vision to the weighty issue of human trafficking. In terse, urgent language, she speaks truth into the emptiness of violation, grief, and predation visited on victims:

> She takes the fruits
> before they even ripen
> to the waterside market to sell
> the way she takes children to the auction ground
>   to be taken abroad
>
> ("Mrs. Gray")

The poet also speaks from the mouth of the abused: "I asked myself—should I live dying, or should I die trying?" ("Eve's Lament"). She articulates in feather-light imagery the pain that accompanies separation:

> Something deep inside me tells me
> I held tight
> to mama's blouse
> the day they snatched me from her.
>
> ("Anthony's Subconscious Mind")

In her engagement with the theme, the poet paints a picture of betrayal on multiple levels: the unknowing betrayal of children by their mothers, as well as the betrayal of a system that fails to intervene. In "A Mother's Song," she speaks as a mother left behind—one left with her questions, grief, and all her worries and hopes for the child she can no longer tuck into bed at night:

> I know it has been so long:
> he might be all grown up, but for me
> he's still my little boy,
> the one I tucked to sleep every night,
> blessed his future, and wished him every good that
> I hadn't experienced myself.
>
> ("A Mother's Song")

Looking also through the eyes of the abused, the poet delves into purposeful betrayals by family or supposed friends, and the startling pain of the accompanying loss of innocence: "each step a reminder of being betrayed / by the guiding star of my journey, / who became the architect of my despair" ("Sydney's Caged Journey").

Deemie does not flinch from the difficult, essential questioning, the ultimate "why" which must be asked by anyone of faith, or anyone who dares hope for more from our imperfect humanity. She asks how it is possible that someone perpetrating evil can pray and be answered, while a victim waits for salvation from the horrors of forced labor and enslavement:

> I hear my master pray to you
> and believe you answer her prayers,
> as cruel as she is.
> If you can answer even the prayers of my perpetrators,
> then why not mine?

("A Child's Song")

The poet acknowledges the complicated tangle of betrayal: that it is not straightforward, and that the path back home is often elusive and fraught with inherent dangers and hidden hurts:

At my new home somewhere in central Monrovia,
I slaved.
Days washed into weeks,
weeks into months,
months into years.

I couldn't go back as a failure to a suffering home
that sent me to suffer.

("Bessie's Lament")

Ultimately, Deemie engages with the betrayal of language: friends that mutate into enemies, husbands who morph into abusers, and families that become the cage that enslaves. Yet throughout, the poet does not lose sight of her goal of reclaiming hope in the midst of betrayal: "I was given no name, / so I named myself Joseph" ("A Child's Song"); "I search for a glimmer of light, / hoping that one day / I will reclaim sovereignty and justice in my own country" ("A Mother's Prayer"). She also writes, "Comfort me with your blessings. / I've had too much of this rain of insults and these storms of beatings. / Clothe me with grace" ("A Child's Song").

Humans for Sale is an exciting new collection of African poetry that begins in lamentation for the involuntary exoduses, sundering of families, and rips in the fabric of community that result from human trafficking. The poet speaks to the fears of mothers for their children, as well as the grief of children looking back at the mothers they left behind. She returns repeatedly to the issue of betrayal, but ultimately turns her gaze to the possibility of courage despite impossible circumstances, and a vision of what can happen when trauma and violence give way to healing.

"Liberia is a source, transit, and destination country for children trafficked for forced labor and sexual exploitation. Most trafficking occurs within the country . . . Children are trafficked for domestic servitude, sexual exploitation, agricultural labor, and street vending. There are reports that Liberian children are also trafficked to Cote d'Ivoire for use in combat. There are reports as well of some orphanages obtaining children through abduction or fraudulent means and exploiting those children in the commercial sex trade or for hawking in the street."

— US State Department Trafficking in Persons Report, 2006

BESSIE'S LAMENT

"Wherever you go,
please don't forget to take care of your sisters
and brothers.
Remember that you have a suffering family that needs your help."

My parents woke me up early Sunday morning
to pray for me and bid me farewell
with pieces of advice
during our family devotion.
I'd leave later that day to live with my new family.

At my new home somewhere in central Monrovia,
I slaved.
Days washed into weeks,
weeks into months,
months into years.

I couldn't go back as a failure to a suffering home
that sent me to suffer.
I ran away from my master/husband.
I ran until I forgot I had legs.

MRS. GRAY

Mother dear
whom everyone favors
has a tree that bears
fruits of labor.
She takes the fruits
before they even ripen
to the waterside market to sell
the way she takes children to the auction ground
                        to be taken abroad
to unknown households in Monrovia.

She makes much profit and does not care.
The seeds of the fruit aren't hers, but those of other women.
She goes back to the farm and encourages other trees to bear
so that she can harvest and nurture them as her own.

"Among children aged 5 to 17 in Liberia, 40.5 percent are engaged in work and 29.5 percent are involved in hazardous occupations, according to the Liberia Institute of Statistics and Geo-Information Services (2021)."

—Freedom Fund

A MOTHER'S SONG

The last I saw him dressed in his Sunday best,
going down the road of fortune.
My boy was going to make me proud someday.
I couldn't afford to give him a better life,
so I entrusted my faith to the fate of the civilized world.

Back home, harvest seasons come and go,
and, like Christ,
there are no signs of his return,
but I still look down the dusty road he once departed on.

I imagine
Saye, my boy, running up to hug me.
I know it has been so long:
he might be all grown up, but for me
he's still my little boy,
the one I tucked to sleep every night,
blessed his future, and wished him every good that
I hadn't experienced myself.
Wherever he is today, my prayers are with him.

A CHILD'S SONG

Maybe my parents don't love me and that's why they gave me away.
I have questioned my existence on this earth.
I was given no name,
so I named myself Joseph.

Lord, may you rain down your mercy if I've in any way offended you
to be punished with this life.
Comfort me with your blessings.
I've had too much of this rain of insults and these storms of beatings.
Clothe me with grace.

I hear my master pray to you
and believe you answer her prayers,
as cruel as she is.
If you can answer even the prayers of my perpetrators,
then why not mine?

I've been shown disgrace.
Gather up the last bits of me:
I've been torn to pieces.
Give me calm.
I've only been claimed by people with selfish aims.
Show me that I can cling to you for hope
and not be drenched
with sorrows and fears.

"Women and children from rural areas are among the most vulnerable, lured by the promise of education, better living conditions, or a good job in the city. Traffickers are mostly extended family members or trusted persons from the community."

—Organisation Internationale de Droit du Développement

SYDNEY'S CAGED JOURNEY

I was happy to see Rissa again after so many years.
She is different now;
I could tell from the piercings and tattoos.

We hugged, cried, laughed, and told all the old stories.
She had served her master long,
bought her freedom, and gained his loyalty.
He had started an agency,
recruiting young girls to go to Oman with her.

I begged.
I wanted to go.
She refused.
I blamed her for being selfish—she left me here suffering.

Rissa assured me I wasn't the one for the job.
I persisted, and eventually she accepted.

Now in Oman, I find myself in a gilded cage,
my wings clipped by the very friend I thought would set me free.
The beautiful streets of Oman, I imagine, are paved with broken dreams,
each step a reminder of being betrayed
by the guiding star of my journey,
who became the architect of my despair.

TINA'S DESPAIR

On a nicely filtered day, a girl walks up and down Buchanan Street,
then back down Broad Street,
scared and bruised.
Selling her body on the streets of Monrovia for her master.

The newly trafficked,
another soul inmate.

A MOTHER'S PRAYER

Six months have passed since I left my babies
to travel far from home for work.
A mother back there, now a prisoner here,
invisible chains are binding my freedom tight.

My madam says I am her property;
trauma grips my heart every time those words slip from her lips.
The fear of dying in Oman clouds my mind.

Trapped in this darkness,
I search for a glimmer of light,
hoping that one day
I will reclaim sovereignty and justice in my own country.

"'You are the only person that lived for 136 days without food,' he said as he looked in the direction of the woman, who sat on a long bench, sandwiched between her husband and other family members.

Bombo also claimed that the woman, whose husband is a taxi driver, voluntarily went to Oman to change her family's fortune."

—Anthony Stephens, "Liberia: Government Loses Human Trafficking Case as Court Acquits Accused Following Dramatic Trial," *FrontPage Africa*, April 26, 2023

EVE'S EXODUS

The day Kwee came,
heaven knew my heart stopped.
Yes—
my new husband came to take me to his new home,
to wed me,
to lift me out of Monrovia's hell.

George, my ex-boyfriend, begged me to rethink my decision.
I refused.
Why would I stay with a cheap and lazy man like him?

Upon landing in Kwee's new country
my passport was taken
so that he could go through the immigration process for me.
We were now a family.
We then drove off to a home
away from Muscat's tall buildings.

I was then hand-delivered to a family who bought me
for a thousand dollars.

EVE'S LAMENT

Inclined to have been bewitched,
the seer said I had a bright future.
Rituals were my future prayers,
driving evil spirits away was my everyday ritual,
making my mind go astray every time I saw a display
of luxurious life.

I asked myself—should I live dying, or should I die trying?
The unquenchable thirst for wealth led me to drown in the cups of my tears.

Now I wish I had wings to fly back to my forbidden past.
I am stuck within the false promises of a man from Facebook,
that his country is better than ours,
that jobs are there in abundance.

I wish I had patience out here.

STORIES OF THE PREDATORY CYCLE

"Why do they beg?" wonders Shirley, a children's rights advocate.
"Where are their parents?
Who would let these youngsters sell on
these dangerous Monrovia streets?"

Susan goes through rural populations
in search of someone to deceive and manipulate.
She doesn't say no to any of the parents' demands;
she willingly agrees to give their children a good life.

If the parents want her to sign papers for taking the children,
she does just that.

The agreement is not lawfully binding.
She doesn't care—
the goal is to make them believe that she's a good person
and have them hurriedly give their children to her.

She gets hold of them,
cuts off all ties,
takes them far away
where they cannot easily contact their parents.
They are now her property.
She gives them new names and sends them to the streets.

HOOK

Hook is not his birth name,
but he is the crook everyone fears.
He was nicknamed because he was light-fingered.
People feared his presence and hid their belongings
whenever he was around.

Hook would be beaten and punished for stealing;
he wouldn't change.
It was his job
to get people's things and report to his master,
an imposter who took him out of his country.

Before he became notorious,
he was a curious lad who longed for adventure.
He did not want to be a farmer like every man in his family.

Now,
to get transported back to Liberia from Morocco,
he requires money to buy his freedom.
He hopes his daily report from pickpocketing
will help him pay for it.

MARIAM'S REFLECTION

I gaze into the mirror.
I hate the person I see;
she lives inside my skin.

Whenever I search my brain for positive memories
to counsel me,
I see him
invading my world.

Four years ago,
I left my family and everything I loved
to come work at Pa Kono's house in Monrovia.
I am now without an identity of my own,
no respect for my name,   working
                                           day in,
                                           day out,
then used by him at night,
then tossed off the bed.

I want to run away from these walls.
My legs have gone weak from trying.
I see someone smile, and it hurts me.
I am alone in my grief.

"The group set up safehouses. But the women still had to escape the agents. The first women to escape jumped over the walls of the compounds where they were working . . . As time went on, the consular official, communicating secretly with M. and the other women through WhatsApp, sent cars to collect them. He issued travel documents. Omani authorities let them go."

— Anthony Stephens and Prue Clarke, "The Liberian women who took on their traffickers and won," The World, August 1, 2023

ANTHONY'S SUBCONSCIOUS MIND

Something deep inside me tells me
I held tight
to mama's blouse
the day they snatched me from her.